THE AMAZING POWER OF
VISION

TURNING DREAMS INTO REALITIES

John Galinetti

THE AMAZING POWER OF VISION

JOHN GALINETTI

© 2019 John Galinetti

All rights reserved. No portion of this book may be reproduced, stored in a retrieval system, or transmitted in any form or by any means—electronic, mechanical, photocopy, recording, scanning, or other—except for brief quotations in critical reviews or articles, without the prior written permission of the publisher.

Scripture quotations marked ESV are from the ESV® Bible (The Holy Bible, English Standard Version®), copyright © 2001 by Crossway, a publishing ministry of Good News Publishers. Used by permission. All rights reserved.

Scripture quotations marked NKJV are from the New King James Version®. © 1982 by Thomas Nelson, Inc. Used by permission. All rights reserved.

Scripture quotations marked (NLT) are taken from the Holy Bible, New Living Translation, copyright ©1996, 2004, 2007, 2013, 2015 by Tyndale House Foundation. Used by permission of Tyndale House Publishers, Inc., Carol Stream, Illinois 60188. All rights reserved.

Printed in the United States of America

ISBN-13: 979 865 455 0057

CONTENTS

INTRODUCTION 7

CHAPTER 1 15

CHAPTER 2 29

CHAPTER 3 41

CHAPTER 4 55

CHATPER 5 67

CHAPTER 6 79

CHAPTER 7 93

CONCLUSION 103

INTRODUCTION

THE POWER AT WORK IN YOU

This book is about one of my favorite subjects: the amazing power of vision, and how to implement vision effectively in your life. Vision is the driving force behind anything worthwhile that happens in the world. Vision sets apart real achievers and winners from drifters and whiners. Vision is what motivates every accomplishment by individuals or groups of people.

Vision is what took men to the moon.

Vision is what built the United States of America.

Vision built every great business — Ford, Apple, Boeing, Walmart and so on.

Vision is behind every successful leader, whether they lead a country, a company or a household.

Vision is something that every person alive must have. It is the only pathway to your destiny and the realization of the greatness that resides in you.

That's why I'm excited that you are reading this book!

Maybe you have caught glimpses of your vision over the years, but don't feel you have successfully implemented the power of vision in your life. Maybe you're afraid of it — or afraid it might not be real. Maybe you don't trust your vision because you're not really sure where it comes from, or how to handle it.

Many people misunderstand vision. They think it is grandiosity, or idealism, or some mystical thing that happens as you are dozing off to sleep. But vision is more practical than that. Simply put, vision helps clearly identify where you are now and where you are going. It is the big picture of your future and the clear concept of where you are headed in your career, ministry, family, and every other area of life. Vision takes a comprehensive look at what is happening now and where you need to be in the future. It then lays out a step-by-step plan to get you there.

Vision touches everything you do, whether you know it or not.

For many years, the subject and power of vision has captivated me, especially as I have seen time and again that all success is primarily the result of vision, not the result of the resources and the approval of men. Whatever call, destiny or direction God has for you, it will require vision to attain it. Vision is more valuable than any other resource you have, and God gives it freely to those who seek Him!

The Bible says very clearly that vision is the fuel of life, and nobody will ever rise above their level of vision. Proverbs 29:18 puts it emphatically: "Where there is no vision the people perish." The word perish literally means, "collapse, crumble, crash, disintegrate and rot." That's a terrible direction to go! Without vision you're not just "getting by." You are collapsing, crumbling, crashing, disintegrating and rotting!

Think about it. Without a vision, each of us would perish.

Without a vision, your business or career will disintegrate.

Without a vision, your church or ministry will collapse.

Those are the facts from the Bible itself.

Yet, tragically, only an estimated two out of one hundred people have a vision for their life. Ninety-eight percent drift through life with no direction or clear-cut vision — they are perishing, shooting aimlessly in the dark, living ineffectively day by day.

My goal in this book is not just to stir you up with talk about vision. It is an energizing subject that gets everyone enthused and ready to go. But reading about it is not enough. My goal is for you to identify and act on your God-given vision, so you will have success and will accomplish something great.

Learning about vision will propel you forward into greatness.

It will stabilize you when turbulence comes.

It will give you a comprehensive plan for growth and achievement.

It will give new meaning to every day of your life!

In this book we're going to talk about:

— what vision is.

— how to receive vision from the Lord.

— how to implement your vision in today's culture.

— avoiding traps that limit your vision's effectiveness.

Helen Keller said it well: "The only thing worse than being blind is having sight but no vision."

If you are ready to answer the call, destiny and direction God has for you, then let's get started. Let's activate the vision God has put inside of you!

Our greatest fear should not be of failure but of succeeding at things in life that don't really matter.

–Francis Chan

Chapter 1

SEEING THE INVISIBLE

I love the old Peanuts comic strip. In one of them, perpetual loser Charlie Brown is out shooting arrows when his friend Linus walks up, sucking his thumb and carrying his ever-present blue blanket.

"Don't interrupt me, Linus. I'm on a roll," Charlie Brown says.

"What are you aiming at?" Linus asks.

Charlie Brown replies, "I really don't know. Wherever my arrow drops, I draw a circle around it."

Unfortunately, that is how most people live — randomly doing this or that, then characterizing it as success. There's a huge difference between hitting a target — or at least coming near it — and simply firing at random and drawing circles around your arrows. To hit a target means to see it and aim for it with focus, skill and determination.

In the first year of our ministry in Grand Blanc, Michigan, pioneering Mount Hope Church, probably few people gave me and Wendy a chance of surviving and finding any success. We knew virtually nobody in town, and we were starting a church from scratch. Outwardly, there seemed to be very little to give us confidence. Thankfully, we weren't living by the outward appearance but by the inward vision God had given us for Grand Blanc — and that vision was much stronger than any discouraging signs.

I remember our first July 4th weekend. We showed up for church in the facility we rented. Because July 4th was a holiday weekend, attendance that Sunday was down to just me, Wendy, my mom, and a friend my mom had brought from Lansing. Service was about to start at 11 a.m., and nobody else was there. My mom came up to me at 10:55 AM. Fear and concern colored her face as she posed a question: "John, are you sure we're going to have church today?" But the question struck me as unexpected. I was getting fired up to preach the Word of God, because I was going to preach as if all the seats were filled. It didn't matter to me that nobody was there. I was "seeing" with the eyes of my heart, and I knew that God was going to bring the increase at the right time.

Still, in the natural, I understood why it "looked" like a good idea to simply cancel the service and go out to lunch together. But Wendy and I weren't endeavoring to walk in the natural. We wanted God's best, and that meant walking in the supernatural vision He had given us.

"Close your eyes, Mom," I respectfully asked as she stood facing me in front of the pulpit. She went along with my request and closed her eyes.

"Now picture this room packed full of people hungry for the word of God," I said. I closed my eyes, too, and a familiar image came to mind — a thousand-seat sanctuary packed with family, friends and people we hadn't met yet. I described that vision to my mom.

"Visualize all those people raising their hands and committing their lives to Christ, plugging into classes, getting healed, saved and empowered," I said.

When I opened my eyes, I noticed tears were flowing down her cheeks.

"Thank you," she told me. "I needed to hear that."

She sat down next to her friend, and I preached in the power of God to those four people in front of me — most of whom were related to me! You would have thought I was in a room of thousands. At the end of my message I gave a simple salvation appeal, and the friend my mom had brought gave his heart to the Lord that day! When the service ended, he came up to me.

"I loved it today!" he said, shaking my hand. He gave his heart to Jesus, all because I obeyed the vision inside me rather than the so-called "reality" in front of my eyes.

What if we had gone by what we saw that day? What if we had canceled service, not shared my message and just went out to lunch that day? There might be one less soul in heaven.

Vision + Faith = Power!

In the biblical Hebrew language, "vision" doesn't just mean what we can see with our natural eyes. Rather, it indicates inward or mental sight — that which we see with the eyes of the spirit. Vision sees things that other people don't see with their natural eyesight. When we believe in that vision, it is called faith. The Bible says faith is the substance that works in us. Vision is seeing; faith is believing what we see (Hebrews 11:1). Only these two things will allow us to look beyond the natural and see ahead to what God wants to happen in our lives.

Did you know that people think in pictures, not words? Vision is the natural language of the mind. Imagination is "image-ination," the picturing of images in the mind. Some believers think imagination is dangerous, unspiritual, or unnecessary. They couldn't be more wrong. God gave us imagination to help us see the vision He deposits in our hearts — vision of what He wants to do in our lives, and what we can accomplish for Him. A God-directed imagination is one of the most powerful things on the planet.

Let me give an example. In John 4:35, Jesus and His disciples were gathered around a well in Samaria, and Jesus was teaching them a profound principle about vision. He said not to just look at a field and "say there are four months and then the harvest. Behold, LIFT UP YOUR EYES. The fields are ripe unto harvest."

That phrase "lift up your eyes" is the key. Was He telling them to crane their necks and look up at the sky? No. Was He telling them to look at the horizon instead of the field in front of them? Of course not. *He was telling them that to succeed in life you need to look beyond what we see and feel.* The physical realm can be deceptive. It only tells us what is happening in the physical, temporary realm which is by nature corrupted, limited and evil. "The things that are visible are temporal [just brief and fleeting] but the things which are invisible are everlasting and imperishable." (II Corinthians 4:18, AMP) The things we see now — our circumstances, problems, perplexities — are "brief and fleeting," subject to change. In fact, they can change in an instant. God's vision, which He shares with us, shows us the ever-present, everlasting supernatural reality which we are to pursue and rely on with confidence.

It is more powerful than the physical realm.

It lasts infinitely longer than what we see with our eyes.

It pleases God and fulfills our greatest life goals and desires.

Think of Peter, the fisherman. Who would have looked at him (and smelled him!) and thought, "Here's a world-changer!" I'll tell you who: Jesus. Because Jesus "lifted up his eyes" and saw what Peter was destined to be in the supernatural realm.

How about Gideon, a fearful Israelite hiding in a wine press from his enemies? Who would have pegged him as a great, courageous military leader? God did! He saw a vision for Gideon that nobody else — not even Gideon — saw.

What about Zacchaeus, the corrupt tax-collector who Jesus met one day in Jericho? Everybody that day became angry with Jesus because He chose to have lunch with a well-known swindler. But Jesus saw him differently. He had a vision for Zacchaeus' future that radically changed the man's life and the community he lived in.

That's what happens when we lift up our eyes! We connect with God's vision. We see beyond the fields in front of us. Real, Bible-based vision lets us look past the natural and visualize what a person, church, organization, business or home can become. To have vision for your life, Jesus insists that you and I look beyond the fields in front of us and see what is possible. Lift up your eyes!

God's vision, not ours

When the disciples "lifted their eyes," they didn't see individual visions of their own making. Peter didn't see a vision of food because he was hungry. John didn't see a vision of a nice, warm bed to sleep in that night, and James didn't see a vision of a lake to swim in. No, our inward sight doesn't spring from our own imaginations and urges. Biblical vision is always God-given vision! We're not talking about the power of positive thinking, we're talking about the power of receiving God's vision and agreeing with Him!

When we lift up our eyes, it's for the purpose of seeing God's vision for us. Much of that vision is already revealed to us in the Word of God. We simply see it in the Word, we attach our faith to it, and we let that imagination grow big inside of us. We "lift our eyes" to see as God sees. He has a vision prepared for your life, your company, your church, your ministry. His goal is to give you the true desires of your heart.

What does that kind of vision look like? Usually, different than we might expect! None of us can conjure up a vision of something we will do for the Lord. "Unless the Lord builds a house, the builders labor in vain."(Psalm 127:1 NIV) All true vision is from Him. He must implant that vision in our hearts and minds, where we empower it through faith. Then and only then will that vision feel satisfying, successful and blessed.

Paul the apostle wrote, "while we do not look at the things which are seen, but at the things which are not seen. For the things which are seen are temporary, but the things which are not seen are eternal." (II Cor. 4:18 NKJV) A major difference between man-made vision and God-given vision is that God-given vision lasts forever! When we lift up our eyes, it's to "see" the invisible which is really far more durable than the present, physical reality. When we lift up our eyes, we are actually shaking off the dust of dead, temporary, earth-bound vision.

Again, Hebrews 11:1 reminds us, "Now faith is the substance of things hoped for, the evidence of things not seen." (NKJV) The phrase, "things not seen" is the key. So many people get excited about what their lives can become, but they want to see it in the natural before they see it spiritually. That's backwards. God's vision requires that we see it supernaturally first, in our spirits. To demand to see it in the physical realm first is what I call "Thomas faith." Thomas the apostle refused to believe Jesus had risen from the dead until he saw him with his own eyes and touched him with his own hands. Jesus appeared to Thomas and the other disciples and told him, "Blessed are those who have not seen and still believe."

All believers know what it's like to exercise faith in the invisible because that's what took place when we came to Christ. You and I have never seen Jesus with our physical eyes, and yet we believe. In the same way, we have never seen mansions in heaven, or the Holy Spirit, or heavenly rewards, or saints and angels in heaven. But we believe in every one of them!

Hebrews 11 repeats this principle over and over, pointing out that the fathers of the faith all lived by God-given vision that looked beyond the physical realm. "Therefore it is of faith that it might be according to grace, so that the promise might be sure to all the seed, not only to those who are of the law, but also to those who are of the faith of Abraham, who is the father of us all (as it is written, "I have made you a father of many nations") in the presence

THE AMAZING POWER OF VISION | 23

of Him whom he believed – God, who gives life to the dead and calls those things which do not exist as though they did." (Romans 4:16-17, NKJV) Abraham called things that were not as though they were. He was motivated by vision to become the father of many nations. He believed and guarded that God-given vision, and it came to pass.

Noah was motivated by things not seen — a vision of the future that made no sense to the people around him. "But without faith it is impossible to please Him, for he who comes to God must believe that He is, and that He is a rewarder of those who diligently seek Him." (Hebrews 11:6, NKJV) "By faith Noah, when warned about things not yet seen, in holy fear built an ark to save his family." (Hebrews 11:7 NIV)

Moses was motivated by the unseen. Hebrews 11:24-27 says he chose to suffer affliction because "he looked to the reward" and endured "seeing him who is invisible." I like what Oral Roberts said: "If you can see the invisible, you can accomplish the impossible."

Did you know that you and I are in the book of Hebrews, too? It says, "by faith we know that the world was framed by the Word of God, ... made of unseen." *By faith we know.* Add yourself to the hall of faith!

Once and for all let's get rid of this idea that we must see something to believe it. The reverse is true: We have to believe it before we see it. Vision is not a magic wand, a wish or a dream. It's our faith partnered with God's will and plans. It's our title deed to His invisible promises. And vision is not visible — at least not to begin with.

THE AMAZING POWER OF VISION | 25

When I think of vision, I have in mind the ability to see above and beyond the majority.

— CHUCK SWINDOLL

CHAPTER 2

WHERE VISION COMES FROM

In the last chapter we talked about how vision doesn't spring from our own natural desires or our unconsecrated, sometimes even unholy and impure imagination. Powerful, eternal vision comes from God Himself! His vision for your life existed before you were ever born. "For we are His workmanship, created in Christ Jesus for good works, which God prepared beforehand that we should walk in them." (Ephesians 2:10, NKJV) The Bible says He created things in advance for us to do and to dream. So how do we find out what those things are?

One word: Prayer!

Vision is always birthed in times of prayer and fellowship with the Father (Jer. 33:3). Prayer has been defined as "The transfer of God's ideas without the stain of human logic." Human logic tends to rob us of vision. We come to church and get all fired up about our God-given vision, and then logic kicks in on the way home and we say, "What am I thinking? I can't possibly do that." That's how logic works when presented with an invisible, supernatural vision from God. Logic simply can't handle the way God works.

That's why there is no substitute for staying in tune with God in prayer. When we spend time with Him, His ideas make more sense to us. We get clarity and confidence in His ways rather than our own. The Bible promises that when we come to God regularly and with enthusiasm, we are always rewarded (Hebrews 11, Matthew 6). And one of those rewards is seeing how (and what) God sees.

Peter was on a rooftop in Joppa in Acts chapter 10, spending time with God in prayer. God chose that moment to give him supernatural revelation that would shake the nations and change the course of history. Because in that moment Peter received an open vision that told him the gospel was not just for Jews, who were God's chosen people, but for gentiles, people of every other culture or ethnic group. We talked about how vision takes place in our "image-ination," and here is a biblical example of that. God gave Peter an image which embodied a principle that changed the entire direction of the church through history. God didn't send a "doctrine angel" to sit with Peter and explain the new direction or lay it out verbally or intellectually. No, God gave him a vision! It's incredible to think about. God so often uses images and pictures to speak to us. He knows just how to communicate with our hearts.

Interestingly, Peter's response to the vision was to be "perplexed." In other words, it didn't fit his human logic. You can picture the struggle he was having because this vision of the future directly contradicted the dietary rules of the Law of Moses. God was saying He wanted to do something totally radical by including the gentiles in the covenant of grace. But when Peter's logic leapt up to defend its own understanding, God had a follow-up plan in place: as soon as Peter had the vision, three men from the house of Cornelius, a Roman (gentile) military leader, arrived. "While Peter was still thinking about the vision the Spirit said to him, 'Simon, three men are looking for you. So get up and go downstairs. Do not hesitate to go with them, for I have sent them.' ... Then Peter invited the men into the house to be his guests." (Acts 10:19-20, 23, NIV)

God is so gracious. He didn't just give Peter a vision; He also gave him immediate opportunity to respond in faith so that his human logic wouldn't wrestle it to the ground. Peter literally put feet to his faith and went with the men to the house of Cornelius, where the gentiles received the Holy Spirit — one of the most important days in human history.

Beware human logic

In the same way, many of us grasp a vision of ourselves doing great things for God in our families, businesses and ministries — until our logic kicks in. Then we wrestle with, "Was that real?" The sad thing is people spend more time in the realm of human logic and earth-bound thinking than with their Heavenly Father. That's where visions die. Only in the presence of the Father do His visions for us make more sense than our faulty logic! Let's be like Peter and get alone with God so we get His image-inations and vision for our lives.

When Wendy and I were expecting the birth of our first child, we had a vision for the delivery that Wendy would be like the Hebrew women who gave birth swiftly and easily. We cultivated that vision and prayed about that vision and stood on those biblical promises.

Then some female relatives visited and shared their stories of woe.

"I was in labor for three and a half days. It was agony," one said. I was thinking, "I can't believe this. We just stepped out in faith, and here's a family member telling us horror stories!" I call those kinds of people Eeyores, from Winnie the Pooh. Eeyores are everywhere. Be careful and don't get caught up in their logic!

Wendy and I decided that their experiences and predictions were not going to move us. We stuck with our vision and stayed in prayer about it. Sure enough, our first child was a quick, smooth delivery. Wendy didn't even need an epidural. We both knew it was because, when given the choice, we allowed God to direct the pictures of what He wanted to do. He accomplished it for us because we attached our faith to the vision He gave us.

How to know you have no vision

Let's do some self-diagnosis here. How do you know if you don't have a God-given vision? Here are a few easy ways to tell:

#1 — You have no prayer time.

If you are not praying, you won't receive anything from the Lord. Period. End of story. In the book of Jeremiah, God said, "Call to me and I will show you great and mighty things." God wants to show you His great and mighty plan for your life, but notice the condition: "Call to me." It's clear that if we don't carve out time in our schedules to call on God, we will remove great and mighty things from our lives. It's that simple. That's when people get into "qué será, será, whatever will be, will be" mode. That's a dangerous way to live, just drifting through life with no direction.

#2 — You think small.

If you ask a typical person what their dream or vision is, they usually say something ambiguous like, "I don't know. To live a good life. Not get sick. Raise good kids. Go on a few awesome vacations. Have fun."

So many people are deceived into thinking their purpose is to make money and enjoy time off. Sports, careers, kids' activities and vacations dictate their enthusiasm and emotions. Leisure, possessions, and in the end retirement, become the goals — and gods — of their lives.

Friends, it's time to wake up! Followers of God must repent of small thinking and small plans. Prayer-less living is small living. Our lives are so valuable, and God has big plans for us to accomplish big things. People who think small are, by definition, not partnering with God in any sort of vision. I like what twentieth-century evangelist D.L. Moody said: "If God is your partner, make your plans BIG!"

Take a quick inventory: Are you hanging around small-minded people? People whose vision doesn't go beyond plans to party on the weekend? Retiring someday? Going fishing on the lake? Be warned — every one of us becomes like who we hang around with. Spend time with small thinkers and you will sink to their level of insignificance.

It is possible, even common, to be a heaven-bound believer and not live by a God-given vision. Our lives can become defined by what those around us are doing — neighbors, family, friends, coworkers. It takes effort to fight against what the secular culture tells us is "normal." It takes being in an atmosphere of faith at church, seminar or in a small group. It takes reading books and listening to podcasts that help us to stay in faith, stay encouraged.

Vision needs an environment of positive hope and faith in which to grow. A place where God's Word defines who we are and gives us promises to stand on. Even the television news can rob you of vision, one report at a time. Have you noticed how programs give you 29 minutes of depressing reports, and in the last minute they offer a positive little story about how a man rescued a kitten? If you are like me, you think, "Thanks a lot for trying to redeem all that gloomy news you just shoveled my way!" Many times, darkness is all they have to offer — but it is hard to keep your vision in the dark. If television, movies or radio are overshadowing your vision, turn them off! What's worth more to you than fulfilling a God-given vision?

#3 — You rely on superstition instead of biblical vision.

I used to work in the delivery side of a restaurant business, and one day I was chatting with a young lady who worked at a deli where I was dropping off products. She told me, "When I pray, I say, 'Twinkle, twinkle little star, how I wonder what you are.'" I couldn't believe my ears. It's amazing the crazy stuff people believe, and they'll even tell you about it when given a chance!

The human soul wants to operate in faith, and when people aren't taught how to live by faith, they grasp onto other things and put their hope in them — weird metaphysical ideas, cults, sin, entertainment, partying, etc. Everyone needs vision. If you don't get your vision from God, the world will gladly supply one.

Some people simply rely on good feelings and they are always trying to make the good feelings last. They learn the hard lesson that good feelings, while enjoyable and a blessing from God, cannot be the source of our vision or security. Circumstances can look one way one day, and completely different the next day. Our vision never has to be shaken.

Before I knew the Lord, I actually used rabbit's feet and horoscopes to try to discern my future and help me do better in sports. I would look at my horoscope and ask, "Does she love me? What's going to happen next in my life?" As I discovered, every vision other than God's vision is a dead end. We are wired for God's presence. "In all your ways acknowledge Him," the Bible says. That means to always look to His vision while not leaning on our own vision, or on bizarre spiritual theories.

One day while Wendy and I were on vacation in Hawaii, we were shopping, and I picked up a lava rock to take home. The store owner saw me and said, "Excuse me. You don't want to take that home with you. You'll be cursed." I looked her in the face — she wasn't joking.

"You can't take anything off the island and think you'll be safe," she continued with a warning tone in her voice.

"Oh, really?" I said.

"Yes," she said firmly. She was basically an evangelist for superstition.

"I'll let you know I have been redeemed from the curse by the blood of Jesus," I told her. "No curse will come on me."

"You're one of those!" she cried out.

"I sure am," I assured her. She seemed to want to flee from the conversation, but she offered some parting words: "When you get on that plane, it'll probably go down."

I shook my head, pocketed the lava rock and promised her it wouldn't. God's vision for my life is based on His promise that I will live long and declare the glory of God. I pictured myself at a ripe old age and continued shopping.

Later, when we got on the plane to go home, I pulled out that rock and the devil whispered to me, "The plane is going to go down." I said, "Devil, you're a liar. I bind that false thought in Jesus' name."

I sat back and began to laugh at the whole idea. Why? Because God's vision is so big in my mind and heart that it crowds out the dumb, fear-filled theories the world offers to try to steal our vision.

We arrived safely in Grand Blanc, and I still have that lava rock. It's a great reminder that the enemy has no power over God-given vision and people who walk by faith!

Where there is no vision, there is no hope.

— GEORGE WASHINGTON CARVER

CHAPTER 3

WRITE THE VISION

My wife Wendy met the Lord when she was in high school, and immediately she found a great church and began to get a vision for her life that was new and exciting. Her home situation was very difficult growing up, but now she had access to God's vision for her life. As she prayed and spent time with the Lord, His vision for her future came alive inside of her. She wrote out forty specific goals for her life.

Within twenty years, *every one* of those forty goals were fulfilled.

Something supernatural happens when you add ink to your vision — by putting it to paper. When we spend time alone with God and listen to His heart for us and our situations, His vision begins to become real on the *inside* of us.

The next step is to get that vision *outside* of us — and write it down. The first place your vision must manifest is on paper! Here's how the Bible commands it:

Then the Lord answered me and said:

"Write the vision

And make it plain on tablets,

That he may run who reads it."

—Habakkuk 2:2 (NKJV)

I love how the Bible gives us such a clear action plan! It says:

1. Write the vision

2. Do so in a clear fashion

3. Write on something permanent (tablets, in their day) so it lasts

4. Let others read it

5. Let others run with it!

People who write their vision down accomplish much more than those who don't. Writing the vision is not just for "goal-oriented people" or over-achievers. Writing the vision is for everyone who wants to accomplish anything meaningful in life. The truth is that we forget almost everything we hear or read after 72 hours. So, writing it down is critical to keeping vision alive.

We could add one more thing to our action plan: The vision must come from God! The Lord didn't tell Habakkuk to write down whatever came to mind. That would have been useless. Rather, he wrote the vision God gave him. It is critical to separate our vision from our feeble or corrupted desires. If you want God to move in the affairs of your life, then your vision must be grounded in truth. The main source of truth is the Bible. Holding up our vision to the light of Scripture is absolutely essential. Everything about our vision must be backed up by the Bible.

For example, if your vision is for total and complete world peace right now, no matter how many times you write that down, you will be disappointed. Why? Because the Bible already tells us there will be no total world peace until the millennium, when Jesus comes back to rule again. Your vision for a world completely at peace right now is not grounded in scriptural truth.

If your vision is to be problem-free in life, that too will disappoint you. The Bible says, "many are the troubles of the righteous, but the Lord delivers him out of them all." We won't avoid troubles in the Christian life, but we will overcome every one of them!

Your vision can't just sound appealing and dazzling — it has to rest on solid, biblical truth. Pray as you write and write as you pray, and always find Scriptures that back up the vision and promise you believe God is giving you. Put those Scriptures in writing next to your vision. This becomes your anchor. Then you can meditate on the vision and the supporting Scriptures, so they become part of your soul. When circumstances look contrary and the winds of adversity blow, you won't cast away your confidence.

You will reference and meditate on what you wrote down.

I'm grateful that my heroes in the faith put their visions on paper. When we started our church, we had eight people and nothing else, really — except for a strong vision. I had caught the vision for my ministry from three main people: John Maxwell, Willie George and Dave Williams. I read all their books and attended their seminars. One time when they were in town I even found out where they were having lunch, and I went to the restaurant and sat across the room to watch how they behaved! That's how much I believed in my vision — and how much I wanted to impact the world like they have.

Like most Americans, I spent my pre-Christian years drifting from experience to experience, hoping and coping: hoping some new thing would work, and coping until it did. Of course, it was miserable. Having a Bible-backed, written-down vision for my life gave me a strong rudder and wind in my sails. Every time I read the vision I have written, I move closer to my future.

If you believe in your vision, you will write it down. You *must* write it down.

Setting faith goals

The next step for turning vision into reality is to break it down into specific faith goals. This is basically what Wendy did with her list of forty goals. A vision is often broader and more general, while faith goals express the vision in steps and stages. The truth is, we probably couldn't handle the vision at the moment we receive the vision! The vision God gives is too big for us – we need God *and* we need to break it down into smaller steps. It's too big and we're not ready. We need to take the journey of faith, embodied in our faith goals.

Every year I take a new notebook, write the year on the cover and write down the things I'm believing God for. I actually have two separate notebooks, one for ministry and one for my personal life. I write whatever I feel the Lord wants me to accomplish this year for Him, and for my finances, in my family, in my hobbies and so on. I usually have thirty to fifty or so faith goals in each notebook.

One year, in the personal notebook, I wrote a goal to catch a big fish. I had always wanted to go charter fishing off the coast of Ft. Lauderdale, so I wrote this in my personal vision notebook and even named the excursion "The Big One."

Sure enough, Wendy and I went on vacation in Ft. Lauderdale that year, and I was able to go out on a charter boat with four other fishermen in the middle of the ocean. I waited my turn, and when the seat opened up, I settled in and waited for a bite. It wasn't five minutes before my reel zinged. The crew put a belt on me and put balloons on the line.

"This is the big one!" they said.

The captain asked me, "What's your name?"

"John!" I said, struggling to keep hold of the line.

"John, you've got a horse on that line!" he announced.

It took me 45 minutes to reel it in, and when all was said and done, I had caught an eight-and-a-half-foot hammerhead shark. The effort was almost overwhelming — but so was the satisfaction! It all started with a vision and then I wrote that faith goal in my notebook.

Mark 11:23-24 says,

"So, Jesus answered and said to them, "Have faith in God. For assuredly, I say to you, whoever says to this mountain, 'Be removed and be cast into the sea,' and does not doubt in his heart, but believes that those things he says will be done, he will have whatever he says. Therefore, I say to you, whatever things you ask when you pray, believe that you receive them, and you will have them."

All faith goals have a specific target. The target of faith in this verse is, "Whatever things you ask." "Things" in the Greek means objects and goals. We could rephrase it, "Whatever objects or goals you ask for." Faith only goes after specific, clear-cut goals. If you don't have goals, then you actually have a vision for failure.

David Yonggi Cho operated in this specific goal-setting all the time. He became the pastor of the largest church in the world, with more than 800,000 people, in Seoul, Korea. But when he began in ministry, he was exceptionally poor. He was single, lived alone and had no furniture. Everything he did, he did on the floor. He ate while sitting on the floor. He slept on the floor because he had no bed. He prayed and read the Bible on the floor. He was also walking miles and miles each day to win souls to Christ.

One day, Cho discovered the Bible promise that whatever you ask for in Jesus' name, you will receive. Faith soared in his heart, and he prayed, "Father, please send me a desk, a chair and a bicycle." Then he waited. And waited. And waited.

Finally, after six months, he complained to God. "I asked you for a desk, a chair and a bicycle, according to your Word," he said. "You know I am preaching the gospel in this poverty-stricken area. How can I tell my people to exercise faith when it's not even working for me?"

The Lord told Cho something amazing: "You weren't specific enough. There are dozens of kinds of desks, chairs and bicycles."

Cho was amazed. Was God really asking him to pray in specific, definite terms? The Lord led him to Hebrews chapter 11 where it says, "Faith is the substance of things hoped for." He realized that "things hoped for" are meant to be specific things, not vague things. So, he knelt to pray again, and this time asked for a desk made of Philippine mahogany, a fancy business chair with rollers and a Schwinn bicycle made in the United States with the gear shifter on the side.

Not only did he pray and ask for these things, he announced to his church that he had them! When some people asked to see them, he took them to his empty office and explained that he didn't have them in the natural yet but was "pregnant" with them in his spirit. In other words, Cho knew they were on the way, just like a baby can't be seen until it is born, but you know it's there. People around town would laugh and mock Cho for that. They would touch his stomach and comment, "Look how big you are becoming!"

But do you know that in time, Cho received each specific thing that he asked for — a desk made of Philippine mahogany, a chair made by Mitsubishi with rollers on it, and a slightly used bicycle from a missionary's son, with the gear shifter on the side.

From that lesson, Cho went on to ask for, and receive, many things, including a church nearing a million people, a university, a newspaper and much more. He taught that nothing comes unless we have a specific vision for it and go after it with God-given faith.

Rules for faith goals

Here are some things to keep in mind about faith goals:

1. They must be specific and concrete

SMART goals are Specific, Measureable, Attainable, Realistic, and Timely. The prayer, "Lord, bless everybody," will never get answered. Neither will, "God, give me whatever you want." Let's learn from Dr. Cho. Prayers that get answered sound like, "Lord, we'd like a three-bedroom house with a fence around the back yard, some trees nearby, a two-car garage and a deck." Or, "I'm believing for this specific amount of a raise this year."

That's vision talking!

2. They must relate to your vision

Some people say, "I love working with children, but I'll make my faith goals about something else." Don't over-complicate it. If serving children is part of your vision, make faith goals about children! Faith goals don't have to be exotic. They should be both faith-filled and practical.

3. They must be written down

While we already talked about this, it's always good to re-emphasize it. A good way to start is to buy a notebook you like in December of each year and start filling it with faith goals for the following year.

4. They should be challenging.

Goals should always focus on things that are presently beyond your reach, leaving room for miracles. Jesus had vision for three followers, then twelve, then 72, then 5,000, then the world.

5. On the other hand, they should not be outlandish, presumptuous or out of touch with God's vision for you.

I've seen some people operate in foolishness rather than by faith, for example, claiming a specific person to be their wife or husband. I'm sorry, but that's not a faith goal — it's infatuation!

I knew of one woman who felt so drawn to a guy who worked at the news station that she had visions of them getting married. The problem was that he wanted nothing to do with her! When it didn't work out, she felt so disappointed that she quit coming to church for a while. I wanted to shout, "That is not what we taught you! You presumed that a faith goal was your ticket to anything you wanted. That's not how it works!"

Another time, a guy attending our church was sweet on a woman who was also an attendee and told me, "The Lord told me she's the one." Again, the lady wanted no part of his "vision" of marriage! I told him, "If it's the Lord, there will be confirmation. She has to know it just like you do." When she refused him, he became embarrassed and discouraged.

Faith goals don't trump a person's will, and they aren't the "get-anything-you-want" pass. They only work for what's in line with God's vision for your life, which is always within the boundaries of God's Word.

6. They should include a deadline

(keeping in mind that delay is not always denial!) For example, "I want to lose 30 pounds in 6 months," "I want to write a book in a year," etc.

7. They must include Bible promises

Jesus compared obeying his commandments to building a strong, sturdy foundation for a house. When the storm came (and they come to everyone), that house stood firm. Faith goals grounded strongly in the Word of God and its everlasting promises will stand the test of time. All others will blow over with the winds of adversity.

When we begin to turn our vision into practical faith goals, I'm telling you, it captivates heaven's attention. God is not moved to action by our crying, our circumstances, or our pain. If He were, all hospitals would be empty, and all suffering would end instantly. Rather, He's moved by our faith expressed in making faith goals that begin to manifest our God-given, heaven-sent vision.

In the same way that faith without works is dead, vision without words is dead.

–John Galinetti

CHAPTER 4

FORWARD-FACING VISION

Vision always looks ahead. In the Bible it's described as "reaching," "pressing," and "upward." Paul strongly encouraged us to forget whatever is behind in life and move toward the vision God has placed in our hearts. "Brethren, I do not count myself to have apprehended; but one thing I do, forgetting those things which are behind and reaching forward to those things which are ahead." (Philippians 3:13, NKJV)

Not once in the Bible does it say to look back with regret! Aren't you glad about that?

Looking backward only keeps you from having forward-facing vision. Peter denied the Lord three times, but he learned to look forward, not backward. Paul was an accomplice to the murder of Stephen. He had to forget a lot of things, including imprisoning and persecuting Christians! He couldn't change what he had done, but he could change what he would do in the future. He developed forward-facing vision.

The Psalmist wrote, "This is the day that the Lord has made." Notice that the Lord made "this day," not yesterday. By the time we get to today, yesterday is always past. God does not live in the past, and we shouldn't either.

Double vision

The Bible speaks strongly against having double-vision. People who have their eyes in two places are unsteady, like waves on the ocean, using a lot of energy but only going back and forth. Their lives are choppy, unpredictable and unproductive. That's why Jesus said it's impossible to serve two masters. In the same way, we cannot serve two visions.

To enter a new vision, we must leave the old vision behind. When Elisha was called by Elijah the prophet to become his student and successor, Elisha left the field he was plowing, slaughtered the oxen, burned the plows and had a great feast to celebrate his change of employment. Talk about nothing to go back to! (See 1 Kings 19:21) The blind beggar Bartimaeus left his familiar spot on the roadside and left his valuable business asset — his blanket — to go after his vision for a miracle. Think about the uncertainty that it caused to walk away from his blanket, which provided him with a place to sit, warmth and a place to catch the coins people tossed to him. For a couple of minutes when Bartimaeus was on his way to Jesus, he had no asset. What an inspiring picture — a blind man walking by faith toward the new vision Jesus had yet to give him.

Do you have that kind of faith to believe your vision when you can't see it yet? Will you follow your vision when it's only an internal reality?

My vision for my life used to be all sports, all the time. I played baseball and was offered a college scholarship. I loved everything about sports. It was easily the biggest part of my life.

The more I pursued God, distance grew between me and my friends because all I wanted to do was talk about the Bible. My vision didn't match theirs anymore. One called me "a butterfly" and said, "You're just bopping around happy all the time." I said, "Why did we go drinking and partying on Friday nights? To be happy! Now I have Jesus in my life and I'm actually happy. Connect the dots!"

Two teammates went to church with me, and one committed his life to the Lord. His dad pulled me into a room after that and asked, "What did you do to our son?" He pointed his finger in my face. A glass of liquor was shaking in his other hand. "He used to be a regular kid but now he wants to talk about God all the time." I couldn't help laughing and he said, "Wipe that smile off your face!" I felt like saying, "What do you want me to do, be depressed?"

Pretty soon, most of my old friends dropped out of my life. God gave me loyal, lifelong friends for everyone that I lost.

Clouded vision

When you look backward, you get clouded vision. Joshua had clouded vision from too much backward looking. He kept thinking of Moses, the great leader, even after Moses was dead. That's why God had to confront Joshua and say, "Moses is dead." Then He yanked his vision around to the future and promised, "I will be with you." "Moses My servant is dead. Now therefore, arise, go over this Jordan, you and all this people, to the land which I am giving to them – the children of Israel." (Joshua 1:2 NKJV)

Some visions are clouded by past sins. We must firmly believe Hebrews 9:14 when it says, "How much more then will the blood of Christ, who through the eternal spirit, offered Himself unblemished to God, cleanse our consciences from acts that lead to death, so we can serve the living God!" When the enemy whispers, "You're a sinner," we can say with confidence that the blood of Christ took that accusation out of commission! Your vision is not about how good you are but how great Jesus' blood is. That clarifies our vision.

My mom was a great woman but was also a great worrier at one time. She claimed to come from a bloodline of championship worriers. That was not an "inheritance" I wanted to carry on! Worry clouds vision. When I was nineteen years old and started to forge a prayer life, I would get up every morning and pray in my room. One morning, Mom opened the door and said, "John, is everything okay?"

"Yeah, why?" I asked.

"Because I hear you praying in here every morning," she said.

"Isn't that what the Bible says to do?" I asked.

"Oh," she said, "I thought something must be wrong."

Speak the vision

Christianity is action-oriented. It requires us to *do* things. It's called the great confession. We must confess Jesus with our mouths. We have to read His Word. We are called to worship, go to church, pray, share the gospel with others, heal the sick and much more.

In the same way that faith without works is dead, vision without *words* is dead. A lot of people's visions go unfulfilled because the vision is never spoken — so the vision stays dormant inside of them. Our world is word-activated. God demonstrated this fundamental truth when he *spoke* the worlds into existence. He didn't *think* them into existence. That tells us something about the power of words. The Bible teaches that our mouths contain the very power of life and death! How's that for authority? In the invisible, spiritual realm of faith, to speak is to activate, so when we fail to speak our vision, we fail to empower it. Believing in our hearts is only half of the process. What causes vision to manifest is saying it. In fact, nothing happens without speaking by faith, however, when we speak our vision with faith, it begins to work strongly in the natural realm.

We must train ourselves, then, just as athletes train themselves, to speak the vision day by day. This brings strength, discipline and focus. Speaking your vision activates the vision! When you speak your faith goals out loud, they come alive in you. When we speak our vision in faith, it leaps into operation.

The Bible says,

"The communication of your faith becomes...effectual...fervent and alive by the acknowledging of every good thing in you in Christ Jesus."— Philemon 1:6

This is one of many promises of Scripture I "chew on" like a cow with its cud. A cow chews, swallows, ruminates, then regurgitates the cud and chews some more. Gross, I know, but that means it's always in my mouth as I go through my day. I repeat it to myself when walking down the hallway or alone in my office. I speak or whisper the truth of God's promises and the vision he has given me. This keeps me anchored to the Word so that when Satan comes to try to steal my vision, he can't.

During my recovery from a jet ski accident which nearly took my life, I surrounded myself with Scriptures — literally. I asked my associate pastor to print out a dozen key Scriptures on big pieces of paper and post them around my hospital room, so I could see them as I lay there hooked up to tubes and machines. My mind stayed full of those promises of healing, and they fueled my vision. I would see myself healthy and well, running again, doing things I normally did. I saw myself on a jet ski. I saw myself achieving and doing more than I had before the accident. I wasn't willing to accept the dire prognosis the doctors gave me. They said I would be in a wheelchair, so I pictured myself coming out of the wheelchair! Too many people passively receive whatever life hands them without going to war for their vision. Sometimes the natural screams that we're going down, but vision tells us we're going up and over!

The Scripture that resonated so powerfully in my heart in that hospital room was from the book of Jeremiah:

"For I will restore health to you

And heal you of your wounds,' says the Lord."

— Jeremiah 30:17 (NKJV)

As soon as the tube came out of my mouth, I was speaking those Scriptures and God's vision for my healing and restoration. I spoke them when alone, with friends and in conversation with the doctors and nurses. They were amazed! It was awesome to see their hearts drawn to God through the process of my miraculous recovery in only one week.

When we communicate our vision to others, it can change their lives, too. When vision is shared with the passion it deserves, people get excited about it. I like how the book of Romans says, "Never be lacking in zeal, but keep your spiritual fervor, serving the Lord." (Romans 12:11, NIV) The Greek word indicates "boiling over" in serving the Lord and going after our vision. Vision can activate vision in other people's lives. It's catching!

Your own words may be the strongest indicator of whether or not our vision will come to pass. What's coming out of your mouth?

A great leader's courage to fulfill his vision comes from passion, not position.

— JOHN C. MAXWELL

CHAPTER 5

PLANNING IS VISION

In November 1959, Pat Robertson and his wife Dede arrived in Virginia with $70 in their pockets and a vision to buy a UHF station in Virginia Beach. Pat raised the money successfully, and the Christian Broadcasting Network (CBN) went on the air in 1961 as the first Christian television network established in the United States. Robertson went on to found Regent University, Operation Blessing and the American Center for Law and Justice. All from humble beginnings — and great vision.

Oral Roberts had just a few dollars and a burning vision to create a Spirit-filled university to teach students to hear God's voice and to go where God's light is dim. Today, Oral Roberts University is a world-class, Spirit-filled university and a pioneer in Christian education. I had a job there and it was awesome. I also was majorly blessed to spend a little time with Oral Roberts himself at his home before he died.

Kurt Warner couldn't get a job in the National Football League, so he was playing on an Arena League football team in Iowa.

Warner stocked groceries by night and played football during his off hours. His vision was to be a starting quarterback in the NFL. Finally, he got his chance and became the backup on the St. Louis Rams. When the first-string quarterback went down with an injury, the season looked lost, but Warner stepped in and guided the "greatest show in turf" to a Super Bowl victory and an MVP award!

Each of these men didn't just have great vision — they were men of planning and action. Pat Robertson moved to a new city and raised money to buy a TV station. Imagine all the work — financial, technological and organizational — that goes into starting a station from scratch!

Oral Roberts University would not exist without the hard work and planning that went into creating it. Oral took action to pursue his vision in the face of monumental criticism from the world, and from other Christians.

Warner kept in great shape and had a plan to reach his goals. He never gave up the God-given vision for his life. That's why he became a Hall of Fame quarterback.

Some people think vision "just happens." I'm here to tell you that vision never "just happens." It always comes with lots of perspiration!

In our journey of starting a church in a city we had never lived in before, I can tell you, planning and action were critical components of our long-term success. Our first location was in a rented Parks and Recreation building. Other groups rented that building, too, and when we arrived on Sunday morning, we were often greeted by beer stains on the rugs, cigarette butts everywhere and the smell of smoke. Even while preaching I could smell the unwelcome aroma of beer and vomit near the pulpit.

One time we had to clean up vomit from a door. The roof and floors leaked when it rained, forcing us to bring buckets to catch the dripping water. The heater broke down several times during winter months, which meant very cold services.

One Sunday we even killed a bat in the nursery. What parent wants to put their child in a room with live bats?

Along with all these problems came the regular set up and break down, things like sound equipment, chairs and children's ministry supplies, that our crews did for four years. That's hard, physical work. But when the presence of God came, we didn't care. We were so thankful to have someplace to meet.

Eventually we moved into a bigger space. What drove us all those years? Vision. Faith and vision allow you to push through the difficult times like we did at the Parks and Rec building. We also learned firsthand how action and planning are a big part of accomplishing faith goals, and ultimately, vision.

Vision happens step by step

God has always worked from plans. Consider the creation of the universe. On Day 1, he did this, on Day 2 he did that, and so on. In Proverbs 8 it shows a master Craftsman at work:

When He prepared the heavens, I was there,

When He drew a circle on the face of the deep,

When He established the clouds above,

When He strengthened the fountains of the deep,

When He assigned to the sea its limit,

So that the waters would not transgress His command,

When He marked out the foundations of the earth,

Then I was beside Him as a master craftsman

(vv. 27-30)

Notice that "He prepared the heavens." Planning down to the smallest detail then led him to act in perfect wisdom as he "drew," "established," "strengthened," "assigned" and "marked out."

It's amazing when you go through the Word of God how highly organized and detailed the Lord is. The structure of the universe, and of our own bodies, testifies to this. Each cell in your body is like a tiny factory much more complex than any super-computer! God plans and organizes everything. He has a plan for forgiveness. A plan for your future. A plan for the Earth to go around the Sun. A plan for providing financially for you. A plan for your family and marriage. A plan for the redemption, healing and deliverance of every person who will receive it.

In Mark 5, we read about a woman who had a bleeding problem, and no physician could help her. When she heard Jesus was in town, she went not just to see Him but to get healed.

"She said within herself."

That phrase is the sound of vision! This woman had a picture in her mind of what she wanted, and then she went after it. She said:

"If I can just touch the hem of his garment, I will be healed."

Picture it: Many hundreds or thousands were pressing in on Jesus without faith. But this woman was unique. She worked her way through the crowd, bleeding, hurting, pushing through people — I love that aggressive faith!

Then she laid hold of his garment. This was her faith goal; the specific, concrete thing she was going after. The faith in her action grabbed Jesus' attention. He turned around and said, "I know someone touched me because I felt power go out of me." That power was drawn out by her vision expressing itself through faith in action.

Think of your faith goals. What is the point of contact — the hem of Jesus' garment — for your vision right now? In other words, what specific action should you be taking by faith? Your job is to go after the hem of His garment — meaning the release of his power — by planning and action. Some people say, "God will do it all. I'm trusting him." No! That's totally the opposite of how God works. We must do our part, so He can do His part. Vision is always a partnership. He can impart vision to us, but we must actually do the planning and implementation of it. If we don't, the vision does not come to pass.

"Do you not know that those who run in a race all run, but one receives the prize? Run in such a way that you may obtain it. And everyone who competes for the prize is temperate in all things. Now they do it to obtain a perishable crown, but we for an imperishable crown. Therefore, I run thus: not with uncertainty. Thus, I fight: not as one who beats the air."

— 1 Corinthians 9:24-27

"I press on, that I may lay hold of that for which Christ Jesus has also laid hold of me. Brethren, I do not count myself to have apprehended; but one thing I do, forgetting those things which are behind and reaching forward to those things which are ahead, I press toward the goal for the prize of the upward call of God in Christ Jesus."

— Philippians 3:12b-14

The spiritual and the practical sides of vision together make us an explosive force for God. They are like a battery which needs two poles to have any power.

After I had been a believer for six months or so, I realized that I wasn't doing anything productive in the church I was attending. I'm an athlete by nature, which means I like to move around and be productive, but here I was attending services and just "riding the pine," as baseball players used to say, sitting on the bench doing nothing. I took it upon myself to start sweeping and shoveling the driveway at church. I was in high school and plenty strong, so I figured that's what I could do. I cleaned toilets, too. I never saw myself as becoming a pastor, but God was looking at my willingness to act and leading me toward an awesome future in ministry. It all started right there with those small actions done in faith.

I wonder now, what if I hadn't taken action and showed a willingness to get my hands dirty and work? What would my future have been?

I know this: if we refuse to act and refuse to plan, we shut down the vision. God will only do his part; we *must* do ours.

Take a moment and think: Where will you be five years from now? What will your relationship with God be like? Your career? Your family? Your finances? If we don't plan and take action to fulfill our faith goals beginning today under the direction of the Holy Spirit, each of us will be in the same place spiritually, mentally, emotionally!

At this moment in time, one thing I am believing God for is $600,000 to pay for Project One, our church's current building project for an expanded children's facility. I am doing what every leader must do and talking about the vision, communicating it as effectively as I can, encouraging people to give and casting a vision for our future as a church. For me, these are the actions I need to take.

We also have a larger plan with various components, including a new 1,000-seat sanctuary, an expanded foyer, and more. Like God did when creating the world, we aren't doing everything in a single moment, but rather progressing through stages of achieving each faith goal. That's how vision is accomplished!

Joel Barker said, "Vision without action is merely a dream. Action without vision just passes the time. Vision and action can change the world." It really can!

God will meet you where you are in order to take you where He wants you to go.

–TONY EVANS

CHAPTER 6

GUARDING THE VISION

I've noticed a trend: As soon as you grab onto your vision and start making faith goals to fulfill it, the devil will send cranky people across your path to say, "I tried that stuff and it didn't work for me."

Don't believe it! Furthermore, don't let their attitude get on you! Agreeing with the right people is a big deal in moving forward.

In some cases, agreeing with the wrong people can cause you to miss the Promised Land.

Moses sent twelve spies into the Promised Land to spy it out. Ten came back with an evil (negative) report, and just two came back with a good (positive) report. All twelve men saw the same land, but ten were too afraid to enter it. They didn't believe God's vision for them. They believed a false, evil vision. The Bible says, "The willing and obedient shall eat the fat of the land." (Isaiah 1:19)

What did the people of Israel do? They agreed with the wrong group! It was a disastrous decision that literally cost them their future. God said that none of the millions of Hebrews would enter the Promised Land — none, that is, except for Joshua and Caleb, the two spies who brought the good report.

Think how close the nation was from realizing its vision, seizing its inheritance, and yet they agreed with the wrong guys. It is one of the most epic failures in all of history.

In another example, hundreds of years later, Israel was experiencing a famine. Elijah the prophet went to one widow and helped her. Was she the only widow in the land? Of course not! There were many widows. But this woman was in a place of faith, trusting the Lord, so Elijah was happy to come into agreement with her. While most people were believing the news reports about the famine, Elijah's faith in agreement with the widow's faith spared her life. (See 1 Kings 17:7-16.)

It's the same principle in the story we just read, of the woman healed of the bleeding issue. Many people were touching Jesus, but only one in that moment came into agreement with his desire to heal. Agreement always produces power. "Your faith has made you well." When our vision lines up with God's, it's literally unstoppable.

We need to agree with God and with others who are walking by faith toward their God-given vision!

Years ago, I had my congregation write their cares and worries on pieces of paper, crumple them up and throw them onto the altar. It was a lot of fun, and more importantly, a lot of people experienced freedom that day. Except for one guy. When everybody else had left, he ran back in from the parking lot, grabbed his crumpled piece of paper, stuffed it into his pocket and ran back to his car to take it with him! I guess he wanted that problem after all.

When I was a new Christian and just beginning to understand that healing and long abundant life are for today, I went over to eat pasta at my grandfather's house. Grandpa Leon was an incredible chef and served for a while as the head chef at the Golden Nugget Hotel in Las Vegas during its heyday. My dad and brother, step-mom and a few others were also there.

Over dinner, talk turned to a certain disease which ran in our family. My grandpa looked at my father and said, "You're going to get it, too." My father sat there and nodded, saying, "Yes, I'm going to get it, too." Both men looked at my older brother and didn't even have to say anything. Before they spoke, he was nodding and acknowledging that he would get this disease, too.

I was next. All three men looked at me. I was eighteen years old and very new to the faith, but something rose up inside of me. I said, "I'm not trying to be offensive, but that disease is not coming on me. I've got a promise that says I overcome by the blood of the Lamb and the word of my testimony. Jesus paid the price for my healing."

My grandfather practically choked on his mostaccioli. He looked at me like, "Who are you to say that?" There was no way I was coming into agreement with them about having that disease. I was believing another vision!

Vision is a corporate responsibility

Just as we must avoid agreeing with the wrong people, we must also seek out and agree with people who share our faith-filled attitude. Your vision is not a solo gig. God designed us to be in a community church so that when the storms of life hit that are designed to take you down, others can help you go higher and build strength into you. Where will your strength come from? God plus you will not cut it. In some ways your vision is only as strong as the community around you.

Some people start out with a great God-given vision, then stop meeting with other believers, and their vision wanes. It's hard to weather the storms alone. Their clear view of the future dims. The Bible teaches that agreement produces spiritual power. "If two or three of you agree on any one thing." When we humble ourselves and embrace the anointing and accountability that comes by remaining in community, our vision stays true. It even gets refined and accelerated!

With what kind of people should we come into agreement? Those who are full of the Word and full of the Holy Spirit! Those who are zealous and fervent for the things of God. Those who speak their faith goals, and speak their vision, and encourage you to speak yours. Those who are willing to sacrifice for their vision. We live in such a sacrifice-averse culture that all you have to do is mention the word "sacrifice" and people's fangs come out. God calls us to a higher place that we can't get to without leaving some things, and even some people, behind. You want people around you who are more convinced of what's ahead of you than what's behind you.

You also want to agree with people who are committed. I have kept this quote by William Hutchison Murray handy for many years: "Commitment is key." Until you are committed, there is hesitancy, a chance to draw back. But the moment you definitely commit yourself, then God moves on your behalf, and a whole stream of events flows forth. Unforeseen meetings, people and material assistance arrive to aid and support your vision which you could not have dreamed of.

I have noticed too, that in the church, individual believers seem to have different levels of faith in different areas. For example, some have strong faith in the area of finances, while others struggle to have faith in that area. Some have faith for healing, some for re-lational restoration, some for evangelism and so on. My advice is simple and practical: go to the person with the strength of faith in the area you need and agree with them for your need and vision!

Belonging to a body of faith-filled, vision-fueled believers is so incredibly important. I saw this up close when I was in high school. My mom had experienced the betrayal of adultery and was divorced from my dad. Then she married a man who was a machine metal model maker at Oldsmobile. He struggled mightily with anger, chain-smoking and alcohol. When I was in 11th grade, I invited him and my mom to church and he was gloriously born again. He was instantly delivered from smoking and alcohol! His face lit up so bright it was like a Christmas tree. Anger turned to joy in his life. I had never seen such a dramatic change in a person.

He and my mom not only attended church all the time, but they both joined the choir! On Sundays, while I stood in the congregation worshiping, they were up front in their choir robes bobbing and swaying and singing. I almost couldn't believe my eyes, because the change in them was so great.

Belonging to that church transformed them. Imagine if my stepfather had gotten saved but never returned to church. Do you think the change would have stuck? I don't.

Resisting negative pressure

Vision is such a major threat to the devil that when he sees you walking into your future courageously, setting faith goals, putting action and planning into your vision and speaking it out, he will start strategizing to neutralize and destroy your vision. That's why the Bible tells us to put on the armor of God. The enemy is plotting against you with great wrath. The good news is he is under our feet — but that victory must be enforced. If you don't recognize his schemes, he'll eat your lunch and leave you a sticky note saying God did it. Then your vision gets eaten up by disappointment and disillusionment. (Remember, God doesn't bring us *into* problems but *out* of them! "He delivered me from all my fears," says Psalm 34.)

One common strategy of the enemy is to wear down your enthusiasm for your vision, so it feels like it is not worth your energy and effort. Most visions are not lost in one dramatic moment but with steady pressure against them, losing steam over time. It can be indiscernible. The Bible says to "cast not away your confidence." It also tells us, "We have need of endurance." (See Hebrews 10:35-36) What are we supposed to endure? Steady pressure from the enemy trying to convince us to stop.

One of the greatest weapons a believer should learn to use is a sparkling, faith-filled attitude of courageous faith and a refusal to quit. Your attitude, more than your aptitude, determines your altitude. Attitudes shape everything in our lives, including our moods, opinions, disposition, personality and reactions. It has been said that confidence, faith, a sense of humor and an upbeat attitude will always outrank brains, connections and experience in determining who really gets ahead and stays ahead. The Bible tell us,

"And be constantly renewed in the spirit of your mind (having a fresh mental and spiritual attitude)."

— Ephesians 4:23 (AMP)

"Do not be conformed to this world (this age) [fashioned after and adapted to its external, superficial customs], but be transformed (changed) by the [entire] renewal of your mind [by its new ideals and its new attitude]."

— Romans 12:2 (AMP)

Faith should shape and govern our attitudes. When presented with negative news, our faith should rise up and swat it down saying, "No way! I believe the Word of God, not that report." When worry has tried to attack me, Philippians 4 has saved my life. What a dynamic part of the Bible this is!

"Be anxious for nothing, but in everything by prayer and supplication, with thanksgiving, let your requests be made known to God; and the peace of God, which surpasses all understanding, will guard your hearts and minds through Christ Jesus. Finally, brethren, whatever things are true, whatever things are noble, whatever things are just, whatever things are pure, whatever things are lovely, whatever things are of good report, if there is any virtue and if there is anything praiseworthy—meditate on these things. The things which you learned and received and heard and saw in me, these do, and the God of peace will be with you."

— Philippians 4:6-9

When I had a breathing tube down my throat after my jet ski accident, I was laughing on the inside because the peace of God was guarding my heart and mind. I wasn't anxious about anything. Rather, I was saying, "The devil's a liar. I've got many more years ahead of me!"

Whenever I hear negative news, I literally tell my heart to be still. "Heart, be still. Mind, close your mouth." I speak to my old nature to keep it from rising up. That evil nature works within the members of our flesh and doesn't want to be accountable to God — or God's vision. We are to "Be strong in the Lord and the power of His might." Our vision is never strong because of us but because of "the power of His might" working within us.

A neighbor of ours used to have an angry little chihuahua that I heard every day. I didn't like the persistent barking, but I have to say that little guy helped my prayer life! I liked the way he wouldn't let something go. He was tenacious and knew who the enemy was. At times we need to get like that!

Several years ago, while mowing my lawn I stepped on a pebble and pain shot up my right leg. The pain was irritating enough to send me to the doctor.

"You have bone chips in your right ankle, probably from your athletic activities as a young man," he said. "We have to take them out, and when we do, you probably won't be able to run like you used to. At forty you'll probably develop arthritis in your ankle, and it'll go up into your knee, and then move over to your other knee."

I sat there listening to the negative diagnosis and when he was done I said, respectfully, "Really? That's an interesting report, but I have a piece of paper that says whatever things I ask when I pray, if I believe that I receive them, I will have them."

"Wow," he said, probably not knowing what else to say.

"Doctor, I appreciate your knowledge and experience, but what you described is not going to happen to me," I assured him.

I had the surgery and afterward was just as active as I was before. I didn't accept the report. Instead, I eradicated every image, suggestion, thought or feeling that did not contribute to my faith and my ability to see myself well. The Bible commands, "Don't give place to the devil." The devil wasn't going to cripple me with bone chips! I would not let him give me that kind of vision for my future!

Operating in faith doesn't stop the storms, but it prevents them from touching our vision. So does agreeing with the right people and surrounding ourselves with a vision-empowered community!

Let God's promises shine on your problems.

–Corrie ten Boom

Chapter 7

THE BUCK STOPS HERE

Vision is meant for every area of life — work, home, church life, even hobbies. Some people think hobbies and leisure are somehow "unspiritual," and that they shouldn't use their faith for anything outside of ministry or family life. Those things are a priority, but hobbies are important too. They represent some of the desires of your heart. The Bible tells us in Psalm 37:4 to, "take delight in the Lord, and He will give you the desires of your heart." Like any loving father, God takes delight in giving us the desires of our heart. In fact, in Matthew 7:11, Jesus reveals the Father's nature when He says, the Father longs to give good gifts to those who ask. Yes, this scripture is specifically talking about the gift of the Holy Spirit. But the word gifts is plural. That means spiritual gifts, and physical gifts, and relational gifts. And even gifts that may not be important in the grand scheme. But they are important to you personally. We serve a personal God. The same faith that works for believing God for breakthroughs in our spiritual lives works in our natural life in areas such as work, family, health, finances, and yes, even our hobbies. Jesus said, "whatever things you ask for when you pray, believe that you receive them, and you will have them." (Mark 11:24)

One good gift I desire each year is a big buck during hunting season, so I wrote it down in my faith goals book: "Lord, I'm believing you for an 8- to 10-point buck to harvest this year." Then I jotted down Scriptures supporting what I was believing God for, including Matthew 7:11, Ephesians 3:20 and Romans 8:32. I declared that a 10-point buck is a good thing! I was praying and planning months ahead of deer season.

Throughout the year leading up to hunting season I would declare, "Lord, I thank you in the name of Jesus for a big 8- to 10-point buck this hunting season." It's also my commitment every year to give the first deer I harvest as a tithe to a pastor who can use it for food. I would picture that big buck walking all the way in from Montana if he had to, saying, "I'm coming to Michigan because I'm John's buck." I envisioned with my eye of faith this beautiful animal coming up to the bait pile where I was waiting in a tree with my crossbow. I visualized shooting accurately and bringing home this awesome creature.

Hunting season began. I shot a deer, the first one of the season, the one I planned to give as a tithe, a first fruit. I had it processed and delivered to an area pastor. Then on the second Friday of October, as the sun began to set, I was in a tree stand with my crossbow, waiting. About two football fields away, in the twilight, I saw a huge deer walking perpendicular to where I was. It looked like he would continue across the field, but right in the middle he did an about face in my direction and walked toward me! I had put out a bait pile of sugar beets, corn and apples. He walked right up to it and my jaw almost dropped.

This thing's big! I thought.

He began crunching on the sugar beets and he did it with authority! CRUNCH! Bucks are so different than does. Does are graceful and elegant. Bucks have big necks, big flanks, big everything. They walk through the forest like they own it.

I dropped the big buck with my crossbow at 30 yards. God gave me the desire of my heart.

Two-wheeler miracle

Here's an example of using faith in a difficult workplace situation.

Before I was a pastor, I used to work for a hotel-restaurant institutional supplies company specializing in pizzerias, driving a truck and delivering restaurant supplies. One of my most important tools was a Magliner, a top-of-the-line two-wheel hand cart that cost more than $300 at the time. Mine was equipped with stairclimbers, which cost even more. A tool like that is everything to a delivery guy delivering 80-lb. bags of flour and working twelve-hour shifts. My company bought me a brand new one when I started.

One day after delivering supplies to a bowling alley restaurant, I forgot to latch the back of the truck when I left. At my next stop I saw the back of the truck open ... and my Magliner gone.

I went back over parts of my route to check gullies to see if it was there. Nothing. I called the chefs and workers on my route. Nobody said they had seen it. Driving back to the warehouse, about 45 minutes away, I retraced my steps in my mind. I just couldn't remember where I'd left it.

So I took it before the Lord.

"Lord," I prayed, "there's a promise in the Word, in Mark 11:24, that says, "...Whatever things you ask when you pray, believe that you receive them, and you will have them." I don't know what happened to that Magliner, but I pray right now that it comes back to me. I pray that it will be a massive witness to all the employees in the company I work at."

Then I went in and told Jerry, my foreman.

"John, do you know how much a Magliner costs?" he asked me.

"I do, Jerry, but I have a piece of paper that says it's coming back in Jesus' Name," I declared boldly. He just shook his head.

"I know you go to that crazy church," he said, probably writing off the cost of the Magliner in his mind.

Over the next month, thoughts often came saying, "That Magliner is never going to show up. It's gone for good." I combated them with the Word and with my vision of the truth: "I see that two-wheeler coming back to me. I don't know how, but Lord, let it be a witness to all the people I work with." I held firm to the victory even as day after day passed with no sign or word of the Magliner.

About a month later I was driving a route when I got a phone call from Mary, the administrator at my company. Back then there were no cell phones, so the call came to a customer in Greenville, Michigan, that I was scheduled to deliver to. As soon as I heard there was a phone call for me, I knew it was about the Magliner. Before I said hello on the telephone, I said, "Mary, share with me the good news."

"They found your two-wheeler," Mary said.

I broke loose in revival in that sub shop.

"Where?" I asked.

"At the bowling alley."

Full of the joy of the Lord, I drove there after my other deliveries and one of the chefs met me with the beautiful Magliner.

"What happened?" I asked him.

"We just found it," he said with a shrug, but I could tell he was hiding something from me.

"What do you mean you just found it?" I asked.

He shook his head but would not make eye contact.

"I'm glad to see it," I continued. "Thank you."

As I wheeled it out the door, another worker ran out after me, looking over his shoulder cautiously. I stopped.

"John," he almost whispered, "I'm not supposed to tell you this. When the owner of this bowling alley and restaurant saw that the back of the truck was open and the Magliner went flying out, he picked it up and kept it for himself. He was so nervous for the next four weeks! I don't know what you were doing, but he was like a bear to be around when he had that thing."

I knew why he was nervous! I was calling my Magliner back into my life while he was trying to keep it, the thief!

"Thanks for telling me," I said, and the man went back into the building.

I was walking tall early the next morning when I walked into the office with my Magliner in front of me. Everyone that day got to see how real faith and miracles work.

Vision for life

Vision is for anything we put our hands and minds to do. It works *everywhere*. As a leader in the Body of Christ, I am always casting vision for people to see and believe in. I cast vision for our next outreach, our next Bible series, our special events and dramas, our church goals and more. In our foyer we have wallboards full of information about what's coming next at our church.

Sometimes, just announcing the vision brings the result. We had a goal to add 125 spaces to our parking lot, but the fundraising was going slow and I didn't know how it was going to happen. I kept announcing the vision and the need, and a guy in our church called me up to say, "The Lord spoke to me to pay off the parking lot goal." He wrote the church a $22,000.00 check and took care of it all!

Another time we were casting vision for café furniture when a guy in one of our Christian education classes said, "Oh, I know of a guy who has a truckload of model home furniture." That's how we got some of our furniture.

I've noticed a strong connection over the years: Finances always follow vision. I have seen it happen for years: Put a goal in front of people, keep it there, and watch the supernatural happen. I like how Chinese missionary Hudson Taylor put it: "God's work done in God's way will never lack God's supplies."

Vision has guided me in my ministry since Wendy and I began. Our first office was in a storage room in the back of an office building. To get to it, you had no choice but to walk through a bathroom. People laughed when they walked through that bathroom to visit me. I would say, "You are going by the throne. Just keep walking." As the church grew, we were able to expand and rent the suite of front offices in that same building.

Without vision, we'd still be in the back office! But vision compels us to move forward. We know we are continuing the story of Hebrews 11, just like every local church that's in the will of God. We're excited about what's ahead. That's vision!

Even now, we are in the middle of raising finances to build our new auditorium and children's wing. I have already visualized myself preaching in that auditorium two hundred times and it's not even built!

THE AMAZING POWER OF VISION | 101

Conclusion

Powerful vision is your inheritance in Christ and the destiny given to you as a child of God! I believe the principles and inspiring stories in this book have the power to change the direction of your life. I hope you share them with people you know, around the dinner table, and in church, at work and wherever you go. These principles and illustrations are like seeds ready to land on good soil. You can actually inspire greater vision in other people by sharing what you have read in these pages.

But I want more than that.

I want you to have miracle stories of your own! I want you to be able to teach others how vision works, and what it is, and how to keep it burning, because you are living a vision-fueled life! That is my greatest desire for this book, that lives and families and generations will be transformed by these simple yet profound truths, and that the transformation will spread far beyond what any of us could imagine.

Would you commit with me to do all we can to walk in higher, greater vision than ever before? **I am committed to this.** Let's live up to our inheritance as sons and daughters of our great God, who has the biggest vision of all!

Bless you as you walk by faith in great vision every day of your life. Amen!

HOW DO I KNOW?

How does a person really know where they go after death? The Bible is so clear on this. Heaven is real, Hell is real and eternity is real, and what you do with the person of Jesus Christ will determine your outcome. God loves you and he wants to give you the gift and the assurance of eternal life. The Bible tells us – whoever calls on the name of the Lord will be saved. Say this prayer right now: Dear Lord, Right now I repent of all my sin, forgive me for breaking your laws and commands. I boldly confess Jesus Christ as my Savior and Lord. I choose to live for you all the days of my life. Thank you Lord for granting me the gift of eternal life. Amen.

"For God so loved the world that He gave His only begotten Son, that whoever believes in Him should not perish but have everlasting life." John 3:16

Romans 10 verses 9 and 13 says that "if you confess with your mouth the Lord Jesus and believe in your heart that God has raised Him from the dead, you will be saved. … For 'whoever calls on the name of the Lord shall be saved.'"

CONTACT INFORMATION FOR PASTOR JOHN GALINETTI

Pastor John Galinetti

8363 Embury Rd.

Grand Blanc, MI 48439

ADDITIONAL INFORMATION AVAILABLE AT:

Address: Mount Hope Church

8363 Embury Rd.

Grand Blanc, MI 48439

Email: info@mhcgb.com

Phone :   810 695-0461

Fax: 810-695-7466

Website: www.mhcgb.com

Facebook: Facebook.com/mounthopegb

Instagram: @mounthopegb

GET YOUR COPY OF *2% CHANCE TO LIVE* AT AMAZON.COM TODAY

LEARN HOW TO EXERCISE THE FAITH YOU ALREADY POSSESS IN JOHN GALINETTI'S FIRST BOOK, *PROGRESSIONS OF FAITH*

ORDER ON AMAZON.COM

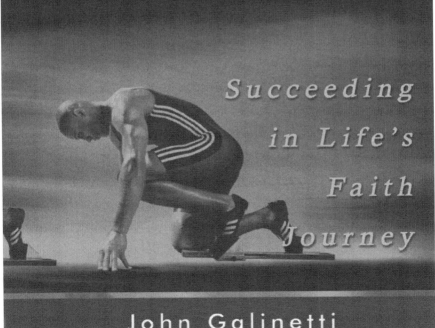

ABOUT JOHN GALINETTI

John Galinetti is the founding pastor of Mount Hope Church, a growing church in Grand Blanc, Michigan. He and his wife Wendy started the church in 1988. Relentlessly, Pastor John has dedicated himself to help people maximize their personal and spiritual potential for the cause of Christ.

Pastor John is heard daily on popular radio stations. His upbeat and motivating program called "The Pastor's Minute" reaches more than 60,000 commuters and offices who make it a regular part of their work day throughout Michigan. His passion and drive is evident as he continues to fervently preach the gospel in 18 nations including cultural centers, packed-out stadiums and sporting arenas.

Pastor John holds credentials with the Michigan District of the Assemblies of God and is a graduate of Global University and Rhema Bible Training College. He has authored two books, Progressions Of Faith and 2% Chance To Live. He has also been featured on the 700 Club television program.

Pastor John is an outdoorsman, and loves spending time with Wendy and their four children.

Made in the USA
Middletown, DE
16 September 2020